www.wadsworth.com

www.wadsworth.com is the World Wide Web site for Wadsworth and is your direct source to dozens of online resources.

At *www.wadsworth.com* you can find out about supplements, demonstration software, and student resources. You can also send email to many of our authors and preview new publications and exciting new technologies.

www.wadsworth.com
Changing the way the world learns [®]

God, Reason, *and* Religion

Steven M. Cahn

The Graduate Center,
The City University of New York

THOMSON
WADSWORTH

Australia • Canada • Mexico • Singapore • Spain
United Kingdom • United States

THOMSON
™
WADSWORTH

Publisher: Holly J. Allen
Acquisitions Editor: Steve Wainwright
Assistant Editor: Lee McCracken and
  Barbara Hillaker
Editorial Assistant: John Gahbauer
Technology Project Manager:
  Julie Aguilar
Marketing Manager: Worth Hawes
Marketing Assistant: Andrew Keay
Advertising Project Manager:
  Bryan Vann
Project Manager, Editorial
  Production: Megan E. Hansen

Art Director: Maria Epes
Print/Media Buyer: Rebecca Cross
Permissions Editor: Joohee Lee
Production Service: Aaron Downey,
  Matrix Productions, Inc.
Copy Editor: Vicki Nelson
Cover Designer: Yvo Riezebos
Cover Image: Getty Images
Compositor: International Typesetting
  and Composition
Printer: West Group

Printed in the United States of America
1 2 3 4 5 6 7 09 08 07 06 05

For more information about our
products, contact us at:
**Thomson Learning Academic
Resource Center
1-800-423-0563**

For permission to use material from
this text or product, submit a request
online at
http://www.thomsonrights.com.
Any additional questions about permissions can be submitted by email to
thomsonrights@thomson.com.

**Thomson Higher Education
10 Davis Drive
Belmont, CA 94002-3098
USA**

Asia (Including India)
Thomson Learning
5 Shenton Way
#01-01 UIC Building
Singapore 068808

Australia/New Zealand
Thomson Learning Australia
102 Dodds Street
Southbank, Victoria 3006
Australia

Canada
Thomson Nelson
1120 Birchmount Road
Toronto, Ontario M1K 5G4
Canada

UK/Europe/Middle East/Africa
Thomson Learning
High Holborn House
50/51 Bedford Row
London WC1R 4LR
United Kingdom

B56
.C33
2006x

Library of Congress Control Number:
2004117745

ISBN 0-495-00507-X

0 60587394

To the memory of my parents,

JUDAH CAHN

whose ideas have informed my thought

EVELYN BAUM CAHN

whose values have inspired my life

C O N T E N T S

PREFACE

This short work is intended to offer a distinctive approach to central issues in the philosophy of religion. I have not sought to achieve comprehensive coverage of the field or grapple with its most current technical literature. Rather, through unusual examples and illustrative materials drawn from perhaps unexpected sources, I have attempted to provide an accessible and, I hope, provocative account of fundamental matters often obscured in more orthodox treatments of the subject.

The book stands independently but can also be used as a supplement to collections of primary sources. It can serve as an introduction to the subject, a companion to a selection of classic texts, or a concluding overview that offers engaging material appropriate for critical comment.

I have drawn freely on articles of mine that have appeared over the past four decades. Some of these papers have been reprinted in collections of my essays or in anthologies, but here I have reworked them in an effort to develop a concise presentation of an overall position.

I very much appreciate the support and advice of my editor, Steve Wainwright. I am also grateful to the staff of Wadsworth for its assistance throughout the stages of production. Over many years I have benefited greatly from numerous discussions of religion and related philosophical matters with my friend and twice co-editor Professor David

Shatz of Yeshiva University. My brother, Victor L. Cahn, playwright and Professor of English at Skidmore College, offered numerous stylistic suggestions. My wife, Marilyn, provided unwavering encouragement and so much more.

In *Stardust Memories,* one of Woody Allen's lesser known movies, Allen plays the role of a troubled film director who imagines various encounters, including one with a group of otherworldly, superintelligent creatures who are prepared to respond to any of his queries. He asks, "Why is there so much human suffering?" The reply comes back, "This is unanswerable." So he tries again: "Is there a God?" This time he is told, "These are the wrong questions."[1]

The exchange is not only humorous but revelatory, for if these questions are intended to shed light on the human condition, then I believe they are, indeed, the wrong ones. But why? If we could be assured that God exists, shouldn't that knowledge change our lives? Wouldn't it provide a foundation for morality and a justification for religion? Wouldn't we gain a deepened understanding of life's triumphs and tragedies?

I think not. In my view, belief in God does not imply religious commitment, nor does religious commitment imply belief in God. Furthermore, in appealing to God's will, we explain neither the world's goods nor its evils. Indeed, to echo the insightful Scottish philosopher David Hume (1711–1776), the existence of God, even if provable, "affords no inference that affects human life."[2]

These claims, however, are mere assertions. In the pages that follow, I shall try to justify them. In so doing, I shall be concerned with a variety of issues that form the core of the philosophy of religion, an ancient branch of philosophical inquiry that attempts to clarify religious beliefs and subject them to critical scrutiny.

My conclusions may be surprising, for although I am not a traditional theist, I find much to admire in a religious life, so long as its beliefs and practices do not violate the methods and results of scientific inquiry. Those who suppose that no religion can meet such a standard are among the readers to whom this book is addressed.

CHAPTER 1

Proving God's Existence?

A THEIST BELIEVES GOD EXISTS. AN ATHEIST BELIEVES GOD does not exist. An agnostic believes the available evidence is insufficient to decide the matter. Which of these positions is the most reasonable?

The first step is to determine what is meant by the term *God*. The word has been used in various ways, ranging from the Greek concept of the Olympian gods to the proposal by the prominent American philosopher John Dewey (1859–1952) that the divine is the "active relation between ideal and actual."[1] Let us adopt the more usual view, common to many religious believers, that *God* refers to an all-good, all-powerful, all-knowing, eternal creator

1

of the world. The question is whether a being of that description exists.

Throughout the centuries, various arguments have been put forth to prove the existence of God. One of the best known is the *cosmological argument*, which rests on the assumption that everything that exists is caused to exist by something else. For example, a house is caused to exist by its builder, and rain is caused to exist by certain meteorological conditions. But if everything that exists is caused to exist by something else, then the world itself must be caused to exist by something else. This "something else" is God.

Although the cosmological argument may seem initially plausible, it has a major difficulty: if everything that exists is caused to exist by something else, then the cause of the world's existence is itself caused to exist by something else. In that case, the cause of the world's existence is not God, for God is an all-powerful being and thus does not depend on anything else for His[2] existence.

A defender of the cosmological argument might try to surmount this difficulty by claiming that the cause of the world's existence is not caused to exist by something else but is self-caused: that is, the reason for its existence lies within itself. However, if we admit the possibility that something is self-caused, the cosmological argument crumbles, for if the cause of the world's existence can be self-caused, why cannot the world be self-caused? In that case, no need would arise to postulate an external cause of the world's existence, for its existence would be self-explanatory.

In an attempt to salvage the cosmological argument, a defender might argue simply that something must have started everything, and this "something" is God. Yet even if we grant the claim that something must have started everything (and this supposition could be contested by appealing to the mathematical notion of an infinite series), the "something" may not be all-good, all-powerful, all-knowing, or eternal. Perhaps the first cause is evil or ceased to exist after a brief life. No such possibilities are excluded by the cosmological argument; thus it is not successful.

A second classic proof for the existence of God is the *ontological argument*. It makes no appeal to empirical evidence but purports to demonstrate that the essence of God implies His existence.

This argument has various versions, the best known of which share a basic structure. God is defined as the greatest of all conceivable beings, one who possesses every perfection. Assuming that a being who exists is greater than one who doesn't, God must exist.

Although this argument has been defended in subtle ways, it is open to the crucial criticism, stated succinctly by the influential German philosopher Immanuel Kant (1724–1804) that existence is not an attribute. In other words, the definition of anything remains the same regardless of whether that thing exists. For example, the definition of a unicorn would not be altered if we discovered a living unicorn, just as our definition of a whooping crane would not be altered if whooping cranes became extinct. In short, whether unicorns or whooping cranes exist does not affect the meaning of the terms *unicorn* and *whooping crane*.

To clarify the point, imagine a ferocious tiger. Now imagine a ferocious tiger that exists. What more is there to imagine in the second case than in the first? Our concept of a ferocious tiger remains the same whether or not any ferocious tigers exist.

Applying this insight to the ontological argument, we can see why it is unsound. Because the definition of a thing remains the same whether or not it exists, the definition of *God* remains the same whether or not He exists. Thus existence cannot be part of the definition of God. God may be defined as the greatest conceivable being, one who possesses every perfection, but existence does not render something greater, since existence is no attribute at all.

To assert that something exists is not to ascribe greatness or perfection to the thing but to state a fact about the world. What we mean by the term *God* is one matter; whether God exists is another. The ontological argument, however, conflates the two and thereby goes awry.

The third argument we shall consider, the *teleological argument*, is much less abstruse. Its defenders point out that the world possesses a highly ordered structure, just like an extraordinarily complex machine. Each part is adjusted to the other parts with wondrous precision. For instance, the human eye, which so many of us take for granted, is a mechanism of such intricacy that its design is breathtaking. But doesn't a design require a designer? The magnificent order of our world cannot be a result of pure chance but must be the work of a supreme mind that is responsible for the order. That supreme mind is God.

Although this argument has persuasive power, it suffers from several critical flaws. To begin with, any world would exhibit some kind of order. Were you to drop at random ten coins on the floor, they would exhibit an order. An order, therefore, does not imply an orderer. If we use the term *design* to mean "a consciously established order," then a design implies a designer. But the crucial question is whether our world exhibits mere order or design.

If the world were just like a machine, as the teleological argument claims, then because a machine has a design and a designer, so would the world. But is it obvious that the world is just like a machine? David Hume, in his *Dialogues Concerning Natural Religion*, argues that our experience is too limited for us to accept such an analogy. He notes that although the world bears some slight resemblance to a machine, the world is also similar to an animal in that "A continual circulation of matter in it produces no disorder; a continual waste in every part is incessantly repaired; the closest sympathy is perceived throughout the entire system; and each part or member, in performing its proper offices, operates both to its own preservation and to that of the whole."[3] Hume further points out that the world is somewhat like a vegetable because neither has sense organs or brains, although both exhibit life and movement. But whereas any machine requires a designer of the machine, animals and vegetables come into being very differently from machines.

Hume is not suggesting that the world came into being as does an animal or vegetable, but he wishes to demonstrate that the world is not sufficiently like an animal, a vegetable, or a machine to permit us to draw reasonable conclusions from such weak analogies. Lacking them, the teleological argument collapses, for we are left with no reason to believe that the world exhibits a design rather than an order.

As Hume points out, however, even if we were to accept the analogy to a machine, the argument still fails. Let us grant, he says, that like effects prove like causes. If the world is like a machine, the cause of the world is like the cause of a machine. Machines are usually built after many trials; so the world was probably built after many attempts. Machines are usually built by many workers; so the world was probably built by many deities. Those who build machines are often inexperienced, careless, or foolish; so the gods, too, may be inexperienced, careless, or foolish. As Hume suggests, perhaps this world "was only the first rude essay of some infant deity who afterwards abandoned it, ashamed of his lame performance." Or perhaps "it is the work only of some dependent, inferior deity, and is the object of derision to his superiors." It might even be "the production of old age and dotage in some superannuated deity; and ever since his death has run on at adventures, from the first impulse and active force which it received from him."[4] By suggesting such possibilities, Hume demonstrates that even if we grant an analogy between the world and a machine, and agree that both were designed, we are not committed to believing that the world's design is the work of one all-good, all-powerful, all-knowing eternal designer.

What, then, is the source of order? The world may have gone through innumerable structural changes until a stable pattern was reached, and the existence of such complex phenomena as the human eye may be a result of the process of natural selection whereby surviving forms of life are those that can adjust. Such an explanation of the world's order not only requires no recourse to the hypothesis of a supreme designer but has also been confirmed by biological research since the time of Charles Darwin.

This reply to the teleological argument may appear conclusive. Yet some of the argument's proponents have responded that the existence of God is not implied merely by the order in the world but, as the ingenious Anglo-Irish philosopher and clergyman George Berkeley (1685–1753) put it, by the "surprising magnificence, beauty, and perfection" of that order.[5] In other words, such a perfect world as ours could not be either the work of an inferior deity or the outcome of impersonal natural processes. Only an all-good, all-powerful, all-knowing creator could have produced such a flawless masterpiece.

This defense of the teleological argument, however, rests on the highly dubious premise that the world is perfect. In fact, the evidence against this view is overwhelming. Consider droughts, floods, famines, hurricanes, tornadoes, earthquakes, tsunamis, and the innumerable varieties of disease that plague us. Is it a perfect world in which babies are born deformed, infants are bitten by rats, and young people die from leukemia? And what of the evils people cause each other? The savageries of war, the indignities of slavery, and the torments of injustice and treachery extend far beyond the limits of our imagination. In short, the human condition is of such a nature that, as Hume observed, "The man of a delicate, refined temper, by being so much more alive than the rest of the world, is only so much more unhappy . . . "[6]

We need not go on enumerating the ills of our world before the teleological argument loses its plausibility. Thus I conclude that none of the three best-known arguments for the existence of God is successful.

CHAPTER 2

The Problem of Evil

THE LACK OF PROOF THAT GOD EXISTS IS NOT BY ITSELF A PROOF

that God does not exist. To reach that conclusion requires

a separate argument, and a much-discussed one is the prob

lem of evil. The Greek philosopher Epicurus (341–270 B.C.E.)

put it most succinctly: Is God willing to prevent evil, but not

able? Then He is impotent. Is He able, but not willing?

Then He is malevolent. Is He both able and willing? From

where, then, comes evil?

In other words, an all-good being would do every-

thing possible to abolish evil. An all-powerful being would

be able to abolish evil. So if an all-good, all-powerful being existed, evil would not. But evil does exist. Therefore, an all-good, all-powerful being does not.

Numerous attempts have been made to provide a *theodicy*, a defense of God's goodness in the face of evil. A promising approach, offered by the contemporary British philosopher and minister John Hick,[1] begins by distinguishing two types of evil: moral and physical. *Moral evils* are those for which human beings are responsible, such as murder, theft, and oppression. *Physical evils* are those for which human beings are not responsible, such as typhoons, locusts, and viruses.

Moral evils are justified by the hypothesis that God has given us free will, the power to do good and the power to do evil. Which we do is up to us. God could have ensured that we always act rightly, but had He done so, He would have had to take away our free will, because a person who is forced to act rightly is not free. God is all-powerful but cannot perform an act whose description is contradictory, because such a supposed act is no act at all. For example, God cannot draw a square circle, but His inability to do so is no limitation on His power, for by definition a circle cannot be square. Similarly, it is no limitation on God's ability that He cannot create free persons who must always do what is right, because by definition a free person is one who does not always have to do what is right. God, therefore, had to choose between creating beings who always did what was right and creating beings who were free to do both right and wrong. In his wisdom He chose the latter, because it constituted the greater good. Thus all moral evils are justified as necessary concomitants of the best possible world God could have created, namely, a world in which persons can do good freely.

Physical evils are justified by their providing the opportunity for human beings to develop moral attributes. If the world were a paradise without hardships and dangers, people would be unable to acquire the strength of character that results from standing firm in the face of difficulties. The world was not intended as a pleasure palace but as an arena of "soul making" in which human beings grapple with their weaknesses and in so doing acquire the strength that will serve them well in some future life.

Hick defends his position further by employing what he terms the "method of negative theodicy." Suppose, contrary to fact, the world were arranged so that nothing could ever go badly. No one could harm anyone else, no one could perform a cowardly act, no one could fail to complete any worthwhile project. Presumably, such a world could be created through innumerable acts of God, who would alter the laws of nature as necessary.

Our present ethical concepts would thereby become useless. What would fortitude mean in an environment without difficulties? What would kindness be if no one needed help? Such a world, however efficiently it promoted pleasure, would be ill adapted for the development of the best qualities of the human personality.

Hick emphasizes that this theodicy points forward in two ways to life after death. First, although we can find many striking instances of good resulting from evil, such as dangers that produce courage or calamities that develop patience, still in many cases evils lead to selfishness or disintegration of character. So any divine purpose of soul making in earthly history must continue beyond this life to achieve more than a fragmentary success.

Second, if we ask whether the business of soul making is so good as to nullify all the evils we find, the theist's answer must be in terms of a future good that is great enough to justify all that has happened.

Does this two-pronged reply to the problem of evil succeed in blunting its force? To some extent. Those who pose the problem may claim that it is logically impossible that an all-good, all-powerful being would permit the existence of evil. As we have seen, under certain circumstances an all-good, all-powerful being might have to allow evil to exist, for if the evil were a necessary component of the best possible world, then a being who wished to bring about that world would have to utilize whatever evil was necessary for the achievement of that goal. Thus no contradiction is involved in asserting that a world containing evil was created by an all-good, all-powerful being.

Yet how likely is it that we live in the best possible world and that all the evils are logically necessary? Do the greatest of horrors and tragedies enhance our lives? Are we better off because of them? How plausible, after all, is Hick's theodicy? Let us test it by considering the effectiveness of a similar approach to an analogous issue I call "the problem of goodness."

The Problem of Goodness

SUPPOSE SOMEONE CLAIMS THAT THE WORLD WAS CREATED BY AN all-powerful, all-knowing, all-evil Demon. Even if no proof of the Demon's existence is offered, the absence of such proof does not by itself demonstrate the Demon's nonexistence. To reach that conclusion requires a separate argument, and a plausible one is "the problem of goodness": An all-evil being would do everything possible to abolish goodness. An all-powerful being would be able to abolish goodness. So if an all-evil, all-powerful being existed, goodness would not. But goodness does exist. Therefore an all-evil, all-powerful being does not.

To paraphrase Epicurus: Is the Demon willing to prevent good, but not able? Then He[1] is impotent. Is He able, but not willing? Then He is benevolent. Is He both able and willing? From where, then, comes goodness?

Surprisingly, we can develop a reply to the problem of goodness along the same lines suggested by John Hick's reply to the problem of evil. We begin by distinguishing two types of goodness: moral and physical. *Moral goods* are those for which human beings are responsible, such as acts of altruism, generosity, and kindheartedness. *Physical goods* are those for which human beings are not responsible, such as sunshine, breathable air, and drinkable water.

The justification of moral goods proceeds by tying their existence to our free will. Surely, performing a bad act freely is more evil than performing it involuntarily. The Demon could have ensured that human beings would always perform bad actions, but then those actions would not have been free, because the Demon would have ensured their occurrence. Simply performing them, therefore, would not have produced the greatest possible evil, because greater evil can be produced by free persons than by unfree ones. The Demon had to provide human beings with freedom so that they might perform their bad actions voluntarily, thus maximizing evil.

As for the justification of physical goods, we should not suppose that the Demon's purpose in creating the world was to construct a chamber of tortures in which the inhabitants would be forced to endure a succession of unrelieved pains. The world can be viewed, instead, as a place of "soul break-ing," in which free human beings, by grappling with the exhausting tasks and challenges in their environment, can have their spirits broken and their wills-to-live destroyed.

This conception of the world can be supported by what, following Hick, we might call the "method of nega-tive justification." Suppose, contrary to fact, the world were arranged so that nothing could ever go well. No one

could help anyone else, no one could perform a coura-
geous act, no one could complete any worthwhile project.
Presumably, such a world could be created through innumerable acts of the Demon, who would alter the laws of
nature as necessary.

Our present ethical concepts would thereby become
useless. What would frustration mean in an environment
without hope? What would selfishness be if no one could
make use of help? Such a world, however efficiently it promoted pain, would be ill adapted for the development of
the worst qualities of the human personality.

This justification, just as Hick's, points forward in
two ways to life after death. First, although we can find
many striking instances of evil's being produced from
good, such as the pollution of beautiful lakes or the
slashing of great paintings, still in many cases goods lead
to altruism or strengthening of character. So any demonic
purpose of soul breaking at work in earthly history must
continue beyond this life to achieve more than a fragmentary success.

Second, if we ask whether the business of soul breaking
is so evil that it nullifies all the goodness we find, the
demonist's answer must be in terms of a future evil great
enough to justify all that has happened.

Does this two-pronged reply to the problem of goodness succeed? To some extent. Those who pose the problem may claim that it is logically impossible that an all-evil,
all-powerful being would permit the existence of goodness. As we have seen, under certain circumstances an all-
evil, all-powerful being might have to allow goodness to
exist, for if the goodness were a necessary component of
the worst possible world, then a being who wished to bring
about that world would have to utilize whatever goodness
was necessary for the achievement of that goal. Thus no
contradiction is involved in asserting that a world containing goodness was created by an all-evil, all-powerful being.

Yet how likely is it that we live in the worst possible world and that all the goods are logically necessary? The answer is that it is highly unlikely, just as it is highly unlikely that we live in the best possible world and that all the evils are logically necessary. What is the evidence that, as Hick proposes, the horrors of bubonic plague somehow contribute to a better world? What is the evidence, as the believer in the Demon suggests, that the beauty of a sunset somehow contributes to a worse world? What is the evidence that, as Hick proposes, the free will of a Hitler achieved greater good than would have been achieved by his performing right actions involuntarily? What is the evidence that, as the believer in the Demon suggests, the free will of a Socrates achieved greater evil than would have been achieved by his performing wrong actions involuntarily?

If this world is neither the worst possible nor the best possible, then it could not have been created by either an all-powerful, all-evil Demon or an all-powerful, all-good God. Thus although the problem of goodness and the problem of evil do not show either demonism or theism to be impossible, the problems show both doctrines to be highly improbable. If demonists or theists can produce any other evidence in favor of their positions, then they can increase the plausibility of their views, but otherwise the reasonable conclusion is that neither the Demon nor God exists.

The Moriarty Hypothesis

THE SUPPOSITION THAT THE WORLD WAS CREATED BY AN omnipotent, omnimalevolent Demon may appear strange. Yet stranger is the realization that its defenders may have the same expectations about the events of this world as do theists. In other words, both demonists and theists may choose to interpret their contrary views as supported equally by any future occurrences, no matter how good or evil they may be.

To illustrate this admittedly counterintuitive claim, consider the fictional example of Sherlock Holmes and his archenemy Professor Moriarty. Holmes believed that Moriarty was the "great malignant brain" behind crime in

London, the "deep organizing power" that unified "every deviltry" into "one connected whole," the "foul spider which lurks in the center," "never caught—never so much as suspected."[1] Now suppose Moriarty's power extended throughout the universe, so that all events (perhaps excluding acts of human freedom) were the work of one omnipotent, omniscient, omnimalevolent Demon. Let us call this theory the *Moriarty hypothesis*.

Does the presence of various goods refute the Moriarty hypothesis? No, for just as theism has been shown to be logically consistent with the world's most horrendous evils, the Moriarty hypothesis can be shown to be logically consistent with the world's most wonderful goods. While any evil can be viewed as logically necessary for a greater good, any good can be viewed as logically necessary for a greater evil. Thus, the Moriarty hypothesis is not obviously false.

Now consider the following two assessments of the human condition:

1. "Is not all life pathetic and futile? . . . We reach. We grasp. And what is left in our hands at the end? A shadow. Or worse than a shadow—misery."
2. "The first entrance into life gives anguish to the newborn infant and to its wretched parent; weakness, impotence, distress attend each stage of that life, and it is, at last, finished in agony and horror."

Which is the viewpoint of a theist and which that of a believer in the Moriarty hypothesis? As it happens, (1) is uttered by Sherlock Holmes,[2] and (2) by the orthodox believer Demea in Hume's *Dialogues Concerning Natural Religion*.[3] The positions appear interchangeable.

Both the theist and the believer in the Moriarty hypothesis recognize that life contains happiness as well as misery. No matter how terrible the misery, the theist may regard it as unsurprising; after all, aren't all evils, in principle, explicable?

To believers in the Moriarty hypothesis, happiness may be regarded as unsurprising; after all, aren't all goods, in principle, explicable? Supporters of both positions are apt to view events that appear to conflict with their fundamental principles merely as tests of fortitude, opportunities to display strength of commitment.

If defenders of either view modified their beliefs in the light of changing circumstances, then their expectations would differ. But believers are loath to admit doubt. They admire those who stand fast in their faith, regardless of appearances.

Any seemingly contrary evidence can be considered ambiguous. St. Paul says, "we see in a mirror, dimly,"[4] and Sherlock Holmes speaks of seeking the truth "through the veil which shrouded it."[5] If events are so difficult to interpret, they provide little reason for believers to abandon deep-seated tenets. Those who vacillate are typically viewed by other members of their communities as weakhearted and faithless.

One other attempt to differentiate the expectations of the theist and the believer in the Moriarty hypothesis is to suppose that theists have reason to be more optimistic than their counterparts. But this presumption is unwarranted. Recall the words from the Book of Ecclesiastes: "Then I accounted those who died long since more fortunate than those who are still living; and happier than either are those who have not yet come into being and have never witnessed the miseries that go on under the sun."[6] A more pessimistic view is hard to imagine.

We may be living, as the theist supposes, in the best of all possible worlds, but if so, the best of all possible worlds contains immense torments. On the other hand, we may be living, as the believer in the Moriarty hypothesis supposes, in the worst of all possible worlds, but if so, the worst of all possible worlds contains enormous delights. Both scenarios offer us reason to be cheerful and reason to be gloomy. Our outlook depends on our personalities, not our theology or demonology.

Thus, as we seek to understand life's vicissitudes, does it make any difference whether we believe in God or in the Moriarty hypothesis? Not if we hold either of these beliefs unshakably. For the more tenaciously we cling to one of them, the less it matters which one.

Dummy Hypotheses

To hold to an explanation of events in the face of conflicting facts is not to protect one's view but to render it pointless. As an illustration of this principle, consider the following anecdote, found in Anita Shreve's novel *All He Ever Wanted:*

> A man is propelled one minute sooner to his automobile because he decides not to stop to kiss his wife goodbye. As a consequence of this omission, he then crosses a bridge one minute before it collapses, taking all its traffic and doomed souls into the swirling and angry depths below. Oblivious, and safely out of harm's way, our man continues on his journey.[1]

Let us first suppose this man is a theist and, when he becomes aware of his good fortune, attributes it to the benevolence of God. What are we to make of his claim?

To begin with, whatever goodness God displayed in this man's case did not extend to the many others who fell to their death. How is God's benevolence compatible with such a tragedy? Our man does not know, but when he ponders the matter, he is likely to suppose that the chain of events serves a divine purpose that lies beyond human understanding.

Next, suppose this man believes in the Moriarty hypothesis and, when he becomes aware of the circumstances, attributes them to the malevolence of the Demon. What are we to make of this claim?

To begin with, whatever evil the Demon displayed in these horrific events did not extend to the man himself, for he was saved. How is the Demon's malevolence compatible with this man's good fortune? He does not know, but when he ponders the matter, he is likely to suppose that the chain of events serves a demonic purpose that lies beyond human understanding.

A third hypothesis the man might accept is that the world is the scene of a struggle between God and the Demon. Both are powerful, but neither is omnipotent. When events go well, God's benevolence is in the ascendancy; when events go badly, the Demon's malevolence is in the ascendancy. In the tragic case under consideration the Demon caused the collapse of the bridge, while God arranged for the one man to be saved.

Is this third explanation unnecessarily complex and therefore to be rejected? No, for even though in one sense it is more complex than the other two, because it involves two supernatural beings rather than only one, in another sense the third explanation is simpler than the other two, because it leaves no aspect of the situation beyond human understanding.

The crucial point is that all three hypotheses (as well as innumerable others of this sort that one might imagine) can be maintained regardless of the facts. For instance, suppose the bridge had collapsed at a time when all vehicles but one had already crossed. The theist would thank God for having saved the lives of so many, while considering it a mystery why the one vehicle was lost; the believer in the Moriarty hypothesis would attribute the loss of the one vehicle to the work of the Demon, while considering it a mystery why the lives of so many were saved; the believer in God and the Demon would thank God for having saved the lives of so many, while attributing the loss of the one vehicle to the work of the Demon.

Any of these incompatible hypotheses can be interpreted to account for whatever events occur. Using them in this way turns them into dummy hypotheses, compatible with all possible facts. Like a dummy bell rope that makes no sound, a dummy hypothesis makes no sense. [2] Its compatibility with all possible situations robs it of any explanatory power.

Contrast a dummy hypothesis with a scientific one, which is typically tested by the following four-step procedure: (1) Formulate the hypothesis clearly; (2) work out the implications of the hypothesis; (3) perform controlled experiments to verify whether these implications hold; (4) observe the consequences of these experiments and, as a result, accept or reject the hypothesis. In practice, complications may abound at each stage. Moreover, the method yields only high probabilities, not certainties, for a hypothesis may pass numerous tests, yet fail additional ones. But the crucial point is that scientific hypotheses are tested, then rejected if inconsistent with the outcome of the tests.

As an example of how scientific method works, consider the case of the American army surgeon Dr. Walter Reed (1851–1902), who sought to control yellow fever. He hypothesized that the disease was caused by a specific type of mosquito. To test this hypothesis, he quarantined some individuals so that they would not come into contact with any of the insects, but did not quarantine the other test subjects. When those exposed developed the disease and those quarantined did not, Reed had strong evidence that the mosquitoes were the cause of the disease.

Had the results of the experiment been different, Reed's hypothesis might have turned out to be false. If those quarantined had developed the disease at the same rate as those exposed, then Reed would have rejected his hypothesis and been led to develop and test others.

That a hypothesis can be disproved by testing is not a weakness of the hypothesis but a strength. Any genuine hypothesis is open to possible refutation. Dummy hypotheses are not open to refutation and therefore do not provide understanding. They may be psychologically comforting but do not enable us to gain any control over our environment.

Some may choose to attribute an outbreak of yellow fever to God or the Demon or a struggle between them. Such hypotheses are untestable, however, and therefore do not help us eradicate or control the disease.

Finally, a few thoughts about the story of the fallen bridge, with which we began. Why did it collapse? The answer is most likely to be found by calling in engineers who can determine the cause, learn from the case, and build a new bridge that will be safer. At no point will they use theories involving any divine or demonic beings.

Yet some may persist in asking why the one man was saved. The answer is that he arrived one minute sooner because of not stopping to kiss his wife goodbye. Why didn't he kiss his wife goodbye? Perhaps he was distracted by thoughts of an upcoming business meeting. Why was that meeting so critical? We can continue such speculation endlessly, but the crucial point is that no question we may ask will be answered satisfactorily by appealing to any dummy hypothesis.

CHAPTER 6

The Appeal to Faith

FEW THEISTS VIEW THEIR BELIEF IN GOD AS RESTING ON A scientific assessment of empirical data. Rather, they see themselves as persons of faith, firm in their convictions regardless of any apparent evidence to the contrary. I have already suggested the pitfalls in disregarding facts that conflict with one's beliefs, but here I want to focus directly on the nature of faith and offer another example to clarify further its inherent dangers.

To have faith is to put aside any doubts, and doing so is sometimes beneficial, since doubt may be counterproductive. Golfers who doubt they will hole their putts almost surely will miss them. Teachers who doubt their students' ability to learn are less effective instructors. A crucial component of achievement is perseverance, and those who doubt themselves are less likely to persist in the face of difficulty or opposition. In short, certitude often correlates with success, whereas doubt is apt to lead to failure.

To describe someone as a person of faith suggests that the individual is strong-willed, fearless, and unwavering. To describe someone as a person without faith suggests that the individual is weak-willed, fearful, and faltering.

Faith, however, can be misplaced. If you are not an experienced mountain climber, but set out to scale Mount Everest because you have faith in your ability to do so, then you are reckless. If your supposed friend routinely betrays your confidence but you continue to have faith in this individual, then you are gullible. If you have faith in your ability to master the violin in ten easy lessons, then you are ignorant.

So faith in the sense of assurance can be wise or foolish. The circumstances of the case make all the difference. But faith in the sense of an unwillingness to acknowledge evidence contrary to one's beliefs is never wise and may be disastrous.

Consider a fictional clairvoyant named Sybil, who is asked to help in the search for a missing friend of yours. After undergoing a trance, Sybil emerges to announce that your friend can be found in a place where darkness dwells. Subsequently, your friend is found tending bar in a Manhattan nightclub. Sybil's followers acclaim her insight because, as they point out, a nightclub dwells in darkness.

You are impressed with Sybil and recommend her to someone else searching for a lost cousin. Sybil is consulted, and after undergoing another trance, emerges to announce that the cousin is to be found in a place where darkness dwells. Subsequently, the cousin is found on Cape Cod. Sybil's followers again acclaim her insight because, as they point out, recently the weather on the Cape has been rainy and the skies dark.

As it turns out, whenever Sybil is consulted regarding a person's whereabouts, she announces that the individual is in a place where darkness dwells. Regardless of the outcome of subsequent searches, her followers acclaim her insight and interpret her prediction so that it conforms with the outcome of the search. If the person being sought is no longer living, that individual surely dwells in darkness, while if the person cannot be located at all, that individual has vanished into darkness.

Are Sybil's predictions true? Are they false? They are neither, for they are consistent with all possible situations and are thus useless, wholly without any significance. Since the place darkness dwells can turn out to be any place, Sybil's words do not identify any particular site or eliminate any possibilities. To use previous terminology, she has offered a dummy hypothesis. Her followers may find that she provides them with psychological comfort. In a crisis, however, paying close attention to her pronouncement and attempting to act on it could be fatal.

Suppose a man is kidnapped and the police need to find out his whereabouts as soon as possible. Every minute counts. Hearing from Sybil's admirers of her reputation for helping to find missing persons, the police consult her and, not surprisingly, she tells them that the victim is to be found where darkness dwells. If the police spend any time trying to decipher what she says and search where she is suggesting, all may be lost, for *we* know, even if the police do not, that her words provide no clue to any particular location.

A similar problem undermines the claim that a certain occurrence is in accord with God's plan, for whatever happens can be understood as in accord with the plan. Such a plan is no plan at all, and having faith in it is akin to having faith in Sybil's predictions.

Believing in God's providence may provide theists with a sense of calm during trying times. In a medical emergency, for example, those who have faith in God may find that prayer helps them deal with the stress of the situation. But before taking time to pray, theists are well advised to seek the services of a reliable physician. For even though having faith in God may offer the best chance for comfort to those who are worried, relying on science offers the best chance for health to those who are ill.

Faith also opens the door to intolerance. If the majority hold a particular faith and are unwilling to be proven wrong, what may be the consequences for a minority? Will the majority permit the minority to believe differently, even if certain that what the minority believes is mistaken?

The historical record is not encouraging. If my belief can be wrong, then your opposing belief can be right, and I am inclined to listen to your arguments. But if my belief cannot be wrong, then your opposing belief cannot be right, and I have no need to listen to your arguments. Indeed, I may set out to save you from your errors. Thus arises persecution, carried out in the name of the good but inevitably leading to a reign of evil. For even though a faith may lack meaning, its adherents may not lack malice.

Skepticism About Faith

A DEVOUT PERSON OF BLAMELESS CHARACTER MAY SUFFER A SERIES of terrible misfortunes. Why would an all-good, all-powerful God allow such injustice? To many theists, the most appropriate response in such a situation is not to doubt God's power or goodness but to assume that the evils would be explicable if only we could understand God's plan.

Surprisingly, a powerful challenge to such faith in God is found in the Bible, in particular, in the Book of Job. Although commonly misinterpreted as a defense of faith in God, the book instead suggests that the more we know of God's intentions, the less they justify His actions. This scriptural story merits careful attention.

Consider the plot. After a short introduction in which Job's exemplary piety and extraordinary good fortune are described, the scene shifts to heaven, where a dialogue takes place between God and Satan. God proudly comments to Satan about Job's great spiritual qualities. Satan scoffs at Job's devoutness, claiming that Job is obedient only because God has given Job good health, a fine family, and untold wealth. Although God Himself testifies to Job's genuine piety, He permits Satan to test Job by inflicting on him the severest personal losses. Suddenly, all ten of Job's children die and his wealth is destroyed. When Job does not relinquish his faith in God, Satan, claiming that Job has maintained his faith only because his own body has been spared, obtains further permission from God to inflict on Job a most painful disease.

The scene now shifts to the land of Uz, the place of Job's residence. Having heard of his misfortunes, Job's three friends Eliphaz, Bildad, and Zophar come to comfort him. Job gives vent to his feelings of despair, cursing the day he was born and avowing that under his circumstances death is better than life. Eliphaz advises Job to calm himself and not despise the chastening of the Almighty. Eliphaz believes that because Job is suffering, he must have sinned, for God does not punish the innocent. Eliphaz also counsels Job to repent of his sins and so be restored to God's favor.

In response, Job points out that Eliphaz has not understood Job's outburst. Job has not lost faith in God. Rather, he longs for death because his life has become intolerable. In a harsh rejoinder, Bildad tells Job that God does not pervert justice, and that if Job were upright he would be prosperous. Job once again pleads with his friends that they do not understand the point of his complaint. He recognizes, as they do, the majesty of God, but he claims to be innocent. He wishes only to know in what way he has erred, so that he might wholeheartedly repent. Finally Job cries to God that he would willingly present his case before Him, if the Almighty would only permit the opportunity.

The three friends and a newcomer, Elihu, repeat Eliphaz's basic argument: Job is suffering and therefore is a sinner; if he would repent his sins, God would pardon him. Job's response continues to be that although he claims innocence, he is prepared to be judged, and if found guilty, stands ready to accept just punishment.

The climax of the story comes when God answers Job from out of a whirlwind. God speaks of His own wisdom and power in the creation and control of the mighty forces of nature. He points out the utter insignificance of humanity in the presence of God. He then questions Job's right even to inquire of God, for how could humanity ever hope to understand the workings of the Almighty? Finally, he urges Job to renew his faith in the wisdom, goodness, and justice of God, even though Job cannot hope to understand their workings.

In the divine presence Job is overawed. He humbles himself before God, promising never to inquire of God again but forever to believe fervently in the greatness and power of the Lord. The story concludes as God rebukes Eliphaz, Bildad, and Zophar for the advice they gave Job, pardoning them only out of regard for him. He heals Job, restores to him twice as much wealth as he had possessed before his misfortunes, and blesses him with ten children and a long and happy life.

Now let us examine the traditional interpretation of the Book of Job, which views it as a defense of God's power, knowledge, and goodness as well as an admission of human ignorance regarding the divine. Here is one such account:

> The Book of Job teaches us that God's ways are beyond the complete understanding of our little minds. Like Job, we must believe that God, who placed us in this world, knows what is best for us. Such faith in the goodness of God, even though we cannot altogether understand it, brings us strength and confidence to face our calamities and sorrows and sufferings.[1]

Again:

> The total mystery of God can be gleaned from the
> Book of Job. There we are presented with a deity whose
> workings in nature can in no way be inferred from a
> knowledge of nature's order. For how did that order
> come into existence? That is God's secret. Nor can
> man's moral intuitions be trusted. Job *knows* he is inno-
> cent, yet in the end he is satisfied to accept the dictate
> that the conventional-minded friends with whom he
> has carried on a courageous, honest debate are in a
> sense correct. Who is he, a mere mortal, to challenge
> God's justice? There is infinitely more to it than even
> his clear conscience can hope to fathom. Indeed he
> cannot any longer allow himself to think of God as just
> or unjust, at least as these terms are understood by
> man. These categories have no meaning when applied
> to God.[2]

And again:

> The positive contribution of the *Book of Job* comes in the
> "Speeches of the Lord" which give Job something better
> than that which is provided by the feeble remarks of his
> friends. The essential point of these final speeches is that
> the problem is too great for the finite mind, that Job sees
> only a small segment of reality, and that his criticisms are
> accordingly inappropriate. How can Job *know* that either
> God's power or goodness is limited? His knowledge of
> temporal things is admittedly slight; his knowledge of
> eternal things is still more slight. The conclusion of the
> book is Job's recognition of his own humble status with
> the consequent mood of childlike trust.[3]

All these variations on the basic interpretation overlook a
key passage: the opening dialogue in heaven. If this scene
were eliminated, the traditional understanding of the
book would be persuasive. Readers would be in the place
of Job. They would not know why he was suffering and

would, like Job, be overawed by God's appearance from out of the whirlwind.

But readers are not in this position. We were told explicitly at the outset of the story why Job would suffer. Satan had, in effect, made a wager with God about the strength of Job's faith, and the wager required Job's suffering. God's words from out of the whirlwind at the climax of the plot appear childish when we are, in effect, behind the scenes. For God to have answered Job's question truthfully would have shown Him to be anything but a great moral force. Does a righteous being make a wager involving human lives? Thus, much in the manner of the bully who, when engaged in a philosophical dispute, challenges opponents to a fistfight to settle the issue, God attacks Job's position *ad hominem,* trying to disallow Job's right to ask an embarrassing question by emphasizing his inability to control nature.

Job does not possess God's power, but Job's question remains unanswered. Job may be overawed, but readers should not be, for we are aware of the circumstances surrounding God's actions. God's ways may be beyond Job's understanding, but they are not beyond the readers'. We can hardly be expected to have "childlike trust" in the goodness of a God who not only punishes Job unfairly but kills his ten children without any possible justification. Had these individuals done anything unjust? Their lives were sacrificed as part of the wager. The ten children who are given to Job at the end of the story may to some extent compensate Job for his previous losses, but are the dead children compensated? Are they restored to life?

What, then, is the significance of the Book of Job? It stands opposed to the prevailing theology of almost all the rest of the Bible. The doctrine of retributive justice, as presented in Deuteronomy, Psalms, Proverbs, and elsewhere, states that a pious person will be rewarded with wealth and happiness; a sinner will suffer both economic and physical adversity. Traditional believers supposed that the righteous were favored by God with material rewards, whereas sinners were punished with calamities. The Book of Job is a criticism of this theology. Later thinkers, however, could not accept this protest. They tried to torture the text into a pattern of orthodoxy. In effect, they turned a challenge to the righteousness of God's justice into a defense of unquestioning faith.

The Book of Job does not justify God's ways; rather, it doubts God's goodness. The book does not provide support for faith in the divine; to the contrary, it offers powerful support for skepticism about such faith.

The Problem of Meaning

IN ATTEMPTING TO EXPLAIN WHY A WORLD CREATED BY AN all-good, all-powerful God contains so much evil, theists are tempted to respond that the reasons are known to God but not to us, for we lack the intellectual powers to grasp His plan. In the words of one of the commentators on the Book of Job whom I quoted previously, "God's ways are beyond the complete understanding of our little minds."

To deny *complete* understanding of God, however, is a dodge, because we may not completely understand anyone, even ourselves. What we seek is at least partial understanding of God. Do we possess it?

To assert that we do reopens the problem of evil, for even a partial understanding of God should include a partial understanding of evil, a burden theists don't wish to shoulder. After all, who is prepared to offer even a partial explanation of how the best possible world contains the Holocaust? The sure way to avoid the question is to deny any understanding of God. To adopt this position, however, is fatal to theism. For how can we make sense of the view that something exists if it is a total mystery?

Suppose, for instance, we are asked whether we believe in the existence of a snark.[1] We inquire what a snark is, what specific characteristics it possesses. If we are told its nature is unknowable, what would be the sense of our affirming or denying its existence? What would we be talking about? Belief in the existence of a wholly incomprehensible snark is empty. So is belief in the existence of a wholly incomprehensible God.

To avoid this pitfall, theists may claim that we do have some knowledge of God's nature, because, for example, we know He is wise and just, although the words *wise* and *just* have a different meaning when applied to God than when applied to human beings. What is this meaning? One possible answer is that no one knows. But this reply leads to a dead end, for we cannot speak intelligently using words we don't understand. If the meaning of the words we apply to God is unknown, then God is unknown.

One traditional response to this difficulty is to maintain that God's attributes cannot be conceived in positive terms but only negatively. For example, to say that "God knows" is to deny that He does not know. This approach is supposed to make it possible to avoid applying human concepts to the divine essence.

But to deny that someone does not possess knowledge is to affirm that the individual does possess knowledge. If that implication fails to hold, then we do not understand the meaning of our own words, and we cannot use them to make meaningful claims.

If God's knowledge has nothing in common with human knowledge, then, as the heterodox Jewish philosopher Levi ben Gershom or Gersonides (1288–1344) argued, we might as well say that God *lacks* knowledge, adding the proviso that the term *knowledge* applied to God does not have the same meaning as it does ordinarily.[2] In other words, once we allow ourselves to use words without being able to offer any explanation of them, we might as well say anything at all, for none of what we say makes any sense.

What if the words we apply to God are to be taken not literally but metaphorically? Does that approach help deal with the problem? Only if the metaphors can be explained in nonmetaphorical language. Otherwise, we are attempting to elucidate a mystery by means of an enigma.

To see how a normal metaphor can be unpacked, consider an example offered by the contemporary Canadian-born philosopher Janet Martin Soskice, who has developed a sophisticated defense of the use of metaphor in speaking of God. Commenting on e. e. cummings's line "nobody, not even the rain, has such small hands," she proposes that "the power of the metaphor rests in its casting up in the reader's mind thoughts of what kinds of hands rain might have, suggestions of fragility, delicacy, transience, ability to reach the smallest places."[3] Thus does Soskice intend to show that a metaphor may offer "a new vision, the birth of a new understanding, a new referential access."[4]

She stresses that science as well as literature uses metaphor. In both cases, the figure of speech arises from a model, which she defines as "an object or state of affairs viewed in terms of its resemblance, real or hypothetical, to some other object or state of affairs."[5] The brain may thus be modeled on a computer, leading to talk of "programming," "inputs," and "feedback."

If, however, theological models are analogous to scientific ones, shouldn't the former, like the latter, be causally explanatory, falsifiable, revisable? Soskice agrees, arguing that "the Christian realist must concede that there is a point, theoretically at least, at which he would be committed to surrendering his theism."[6] But where is this point? The question is invariably left unanswered.

In offering her account of cummings's line, Soskice explains its metaphor in nonmetaphorical language. After she does so, the metaphor yields the nonmetaphorical assertion that the rain is delicate and transient. If that rain is part of a major hurricane, then the claim is false.

Can theological metaphors also be explained so as to yield nonmetaphorical claims? If so, we can speak of God literally, a position theists seek to deny.

But if the metaphors cannot be explained, why is one more appropriate than another? We talk of God the Father or, possibly, God the Mother. But why not God the Aunt or Uncle, God the Cousin, or God the Neighbor? Some may protest that these phrases are inexplicable. Perhaps so. But one inexplicable metaphor is as good as another.

Thus we are left with the problem of meaning: How can we describe an indescribable God?

CHAPTER 9

Miracles

IF WE CANNOT SPEAK OF GOD, CAN WE AT LEAST EXPERIENCE THE workings of His will? Do some events bear the stamp of divine intervention?

Return to the case of the man who crosses a bridge one minute before it collapses. Let us alter the circumstances and suppose the man is driving on the bridge when the tragedy occurs. No one on the bridge survives, except for him. He is thrown from his car, lands in soft soil, and is unharmed. Has a miracle occurred?

In one sense of the word it has, for a miracle may be understood as an unexpected, wonderful event, and the man's escape from death is in that sense miraculous. But is it miraculous in a stronger sense of the word—is it an act of God that suspends the laws of nature?

Some theists may be tempted to believe so, especially when several members of a local church come forward to say that as they were watching the events unfold, they saw a fiery chariot appear from the heavens, pick up the man as he was falling, and bring him safely to earth.[1] Do their reports increase the likelihood that a miracle occurred?

Testimony offered in court is subject to cross-examination and may turn out to be mistaken. Assume two witnesses say that they observed the defendant Smith commit a robbery. Yet forty reliable others are prepared to testify that at the time in question Smith was playing in a volleyball game many miles away. So the two witnesses who thought they saw Smith commit the crime were apparently mistaken. When challenged, though, the two insist they couldn't be wrong because they certainly seemed to see Smith.

To assess their claim we need to draw a distinction between statements such as "I see a star" and statements such as "I seem to see a star." If I see a star, then a star is present for me to see. I may be wrong that I am seeing a star, for perhaps I am seeing an airplane instead, but if I am right that I am seeing a star, the truth of my statement implies the existence of a star. If it turns out that I only thought I was seeing a star, but in fact I was seeing an airplane, I can still claim that I *seemed* to see a star. In making that claim sincerely, I am safe from error, but my saying that I seemed to see something doesn't imply the existence of what I seemed to see. In other words, statements such as "I see a star" may be false, but if they are true, they imply the existence of the thing perceived. Statements such as "I seem to see a star," if sincere, cannot be false but do not imply the existence of the thing seemingly perceived.

Confusion sets in if some persons claim that a thing exists because they seem to see it. What is necessary is that *if* they see something, it is present. What is also necessary is that if they *seem* to see something, they can't be wrong that they *seem* to see it; they can, however, be wrong that it is present.

In the case of the witnesses who seemed to see Smith commit the robbery, did they actually see what they thought they saw? To determine the reliability of a person's testimony, we assess it in light of answers to questions such as: (1) How many witnesses saw the event? (2) Do the witnesses agree in all important respects? (3) Are they widely regarded as persons of reliable judgment? (4) Do they have any reason to want to see what they claim to have seen? (5) Is anyone trying to mislead them? (6) Is their testimony incompatible with other evidence? (7) How likely is their testimony compared to the likelihood of any widely accepted views with which it is incompatible? (8) How plausible is an alternative explanation of why they seemed to see what they thought they saw?

In Smith's case, forty witnesses testify that they saw him playing volleyball, whereas only two say they saw him commit the robbery. Let us presume that the testimony of the forty is in all important respects identical, that they are reliable persons with no reason to lie, that no one is trying to mislead them, that their testimony fits all the facts except for the accounts of the two dissenting witnesses, that the testimony of the forty is not incompatible with any laws of nature or other widely believed claims, and that Smith has an identical twin brother who doesn't play volleyball but has previously been convicted of crimes and was known to be in the vicinity of the crime scene when the robbery occurred. Given all these factors, any reasonable jury would find Smith "not guilty."

Let us now use these same criteria to judge the plausibility of those who reported seeing a fiery chariot save the man falling from the bridge. The number of witnesses was small, probably they each described the chariot somewhat differently, their reliability may be suspect in view of their previous accounts of equally strange sightings, their commitment to a particular type of theism may give them reason to wish to witness miracles, they may be subject to the will of a leader who praises them for reporting supposed miracles, and no traces of any chariot tracks are found in the ground where the man came to rest.

Most important, however, their reports imply the suspension of the law of gravity, a law as highly confirmed as any could be. So the weight of the evidence suggests not that the law ceased to operate but that these observers made a mistake.

As to how they were misled, we might suppose that remains of a burning car are found near where the man landed, and these burning parts might have been mistaken for a chariot. Granted, this hypothesis is not highly plausible, but it is far more so than the possibility that the law of gravity was suspended while a fiery chariot appeared and disappeared.

Admittedly, I have stacked the deck against those reporting the miracle by assuming weaknesses in their testimony that may not fit the facts in every case. Suppose the witnesses were more numerous, independent, and reliable. Would such conditions increase the probability that a miracle occurred?

Not to a significant degree, for as Hume noted in his much-discussed account of miracles, "There must . . . be a uniform experience against every miraculous event, otherwise the event would not merit that appellation. And as a uniform experience amounts to a proof, there is here a direct and full *proof*, from the nature of the fact, against the existence of any miracle . . ."[2] In other words, because a miracle suspends a natural law, and because the evidence for the operation of such laws is overwhelming, the probability that a miracle occurred is always far less than the probability that the law suddenly stopped functioning. Thus invariably any report of a miracle is highly unlikely.

Theists are most tempted to believe in a miracle when it involves the triumph of good over evil. If the man saved in the collapse of the bridge was of saintly character whereas those killed in the accident were seeking to harm him, then considering the event miraculous is nearly irresistible. But to assume that God acts so that the good prosper while evildoers are punished is to agree with Job's friends, whom God rebuked for their mistaken views. After all, if we attribute wondrous events to God, who is supposed to be responsible for horrendous ones?

CHAPTER 10

God Without Religion

SO FAR I HAVE FOCUSED ON BELIEF IN GOD WITHOUT MAKING ANY reference to religious commitment. Yet often theism and religiosity are treated as equivalent. For example, a public opinion survey may ask Americans whether they believe in God and, when a high percentage say they do, the results are said to show that a high percentage of Americans are religious. This conclusion, however, is not implied by the data.

To see why, suppose that contrary to what most philosophers believe, the cosmological, ontological, and teleological arguments for the existence of God are all sound. Let us grant the existence of the most perfect conceivable being, the all-good, all-powerful creator of the universe. What implications follow from this premise that would suggest participation in any religion?

Some people would feel more secure in the knowledge that the world had been planned by an all-good being. Others would feel insecure, realizing the extent to which their existence depended on a decision of this being. In any case, most people, either out of fear or respect, would wish to act in accord with God's will.

None of the arguments for believing in God, however, provides any hint as to which actions God wishes us to perform or what we ought to do to please or obey Him. We may affirm that God is all-good yet have no way of knowing the highest moral standards. All we may presume is that, whatever these standards, God always acts in accordance with them. We might expect God to have implanted the correct moral intuitions in our minds, but this supposition is doubtful in view of the conflicts among people's intuitions. Furthermore, even if a consensus prevailed, it might be only a means by which God tests us to see whether we have the courage to dissent from popular opinion.

Some would argue that if God exists, then at least it follows that murder is immoral, because it would be immoral to destroy what God in His infinite wisdom created. This argument, however, fails on several grounds. First, God also created germs, viruses, and disease-carrying rats. Does it follow that because God created these things they ought not be eliminated? Second, if God arranged for us to live, He also arranged for us to die. Does it follow that by killing we are assisting the work of God? Third, God provided us with the mental and physical potential to commit murder. Does it follow that God wishes us to fulfill this potential?

To attempt to deduce moral precepts from God's existence is to try to deduce normative conclusions from purely factual premises, a move Hume showed to be logically impossible.[1] No such deduction is valid, and thus any moral principle is consistent with the existence of God.

Because the arguments for believing in God afford no means of distinguishing good from evil, no person can be sure how to obey God and do what is best in His eyes. We may hope our actions are in accord with God's standards, but no test is available to check. Some seemingly good persons suffer great ills, while some seemingly evil persons achieve great happiness. Perhaps in a future life these outcomes are reversed, but we have no way of ascertaining who, if anyone, is ultimately punished and who ultimately rewarded.

Over the course of history, those who believed in God's existence typically were eager to learn His will and tended to rely on those individuals who claimed to possess such insight. Diviners, seers, and priests were given positions of great influence. Competition among them was severe, for no one could be sure which oracle to believe.

In any case, prophets died, and their supposedly revelatory powers disappeared with them. For practical purposes, what was needed was a permanent record of God's will. This requirement was met by the writing of holy books in which God's will was revealed for all to know.

But even though many such books were supposed to embody the will of God, they conflicted with one another. Which was to be believed? Theism by itself yields no answer. The only direct avenue to the divine will is a personal, self-validating experience in which one senses the presence of God and apprehends which of the putative holy books is genuine.

Drawing on a distinction made in the discussion of miracles, however, we need to distinguish between seeming to see God and seeing God. Anyone may claim to have seemed to see God, and we ordinarily have no reason to doubt that the person did *seem* to see the divine. But such testimony is fallible; it does not prove that the person saw God. As the incisive American philosopher Sidney Hook (1902–1989) wrote, "Whether an actual angel speaks to me in my beatific vision or whether I only dreamed he spoke, the truth of what he says can only be tested in the same way as I test what my neighbor says to me. For even my neighbor may claim to be a messenger of the Lord."[2] Testimony of revelations, like testimony of miracles, has to meet standards of reliability. Yet claims to have seen and heard God are invariably dubious, especially since they imply the suspension of accepted laws of nature related to optics and acoustics, and for that reason alone are highly implausible.

Suppose you are convinced that God exists but are not persuaded that anyone knows His will. In that case you might choose not to practice any religion. Your position would be coherent and best described as that of a nonreligious theist or, to use a term popular in the seventeenth and eighteenth centuries, a deist. Among those who held this view were Benjamin Franklin, George Washington, and Thomas Jefferson, an estimable group indeed.

Playing the Odds

ASSUMING WE AGREE WITH THOSE WHO DENY INSIGHT INTO GOD'S will, might prudence nevertheless dictate that we participate in an established religion, because each offers a well-trodden path to understanding the divine? Isn't it likely that millions of believers are on the right track to truth? Even if they are not, what has been lost by joining them and trying their ways?

This line of argument is similar to *Pascal's wager,* the reasoning offered by the French mathematician and religious philosopher Blaise Pascal (1623–1662), for why one should believe in God even without any proof of His existence. Pascal argues that if you believe, and God exists, then you attain heavenly bliss; if you believe, and God doesn't exist, little is lost. On the other hand, if you don't believe, and God does exist, then you are doomed to the torments of damnation; if you don't believe, and God doesn't exist, little is gained. Thus belief is the safest strategy.[1]

Pascal, however, failed to consider the possibility that a different kind of God might exist, for example, one who wishes us to hold only those beliefs supported by the available evidence. If such a God exists, then in the absence of evidence, *not* believing is the safest strategy.

A similar difficulty undermines the supposition that in the absence of knowledge about God, the safest strategy is to join a religion, worship God, pray to Him, and hope for the best. After all, suppose God doesn't approve of any religion and doesn't wish to be worshipped or prayed to. What if He rewards those who shun such activities? In that case, avoiding them is the safest strategy.

Admittedly, this account of the divine nature is contrary to what many people suppose. They take as obvious that God wishes to receive our veneration and supplications. But leaving aside for a moment the incomprehensibility of God, which would make it impossible for anyone to know His nature, let me offer an analogy to suggest that what God wills may be contrary to widespread expectations.

Most children, although sadly not all, enter this world beloved by their parents who, having created them, make every effort to nurture and support them, sometimes even at great cost to the parents' own ambitions. In response, the children may dearly love one or both of their parents, not merely honoring them in accord with the biblical injunction, but adoring them.

Yet sensible parents would not wish to be the object of their children's worship. To the contrary, they would find the situation distressing and believe that in some way they had failed as parents, for even though they welcomed the love of an independent child who had learned to make decisions and take responsibilities, they did not seek nor would they want the single-minded devotion of a dependent child who relied on them for all decisions and was unwilling to shoulder any responsibilities.

If we are children of God, might not God, like a wise parent, wish those He created to be independent, not dependent? Might He disapprove of being worshipped at public services and prayed to at times of hardship? Might He instead favor those who meditated privately, if at all, performed good deeds rather than godly rituals, and displayed the fortitude to persevere in the face of difficulties without appealing for His help? Perhaps, as Benjamin Franklin wrote, "God helps them who help themselves."[2] Indeed, God's will may have been best understood by the prophet Amos, when he attributed to Him the following words:

I loathe, I spurn your festivals,
I am not appeased by your solemn
    assemblies.
If you offer Me burnt offerings—or
    your meal offerings—
I will not accept them;
I will pay no heed
To your gifts of fatlings.
Spare Me the sound of your hymns,
And let Me not hear the music of
    your lutes.
But let justice well up like water,
Righteousness like an unfailing stream.[3]

Thus, rather than venerating God and offering Him supplications, we should focus our efforts on being considerate to others.

Granted, I have been speculating about matters that may lie beyond human understanding. If they do not, I believe my account of God's will is as plausible as another's. But if grasping the nature of the divine is impossible, then joining an established religion in an effort to find the truth is no more reasonable than not joining. In the absence of any relevant information, all bets are off.

Religions

In the last chapter, I considered the decision to accept a religion as if the choice among religions did not matter. But the divergences among them are vast, including different rituals, different prayers, different theistic systems, and different moral beliefs.[1]

Judaism believes in a unitary god, Zoroastrianism in two gods, Christianity in a triune god, Shinto in gods too numerous to count; Theravada Buddhism and Samkhya and Mimamsa Hinduism believe in no god at all. The Confucian Mencius teaches that human nature is essentially good; Christians view human nature as tainted by original sin. Hindus consider the soul immortal; Buddhists view it as impermanent. Christians place a heavy emphasis on an afterlife; the central concern of Judaism is life in this world. Moslems practice *purdah*, the seclusion of women; in Shinto female priests conduct religious ceremonies. The Sikh religion is unique in requiring its members to have long hair, a bracelet, a dagger, a comb, and short pants.

Indeed, every belief and practice of any particular religion is rejected by some other religions. Furthermore, although each religion has its own holy writings that are thought to embody the divine will as revealed to inspired prophets, within each religion interpretations of scripture differ and have frequently given rise to fierce internal doctrinal disputes. Recall that despite the many matters about which Protestants and Catholics agree, their disagreements have led to centuries of bloodshed.

Such differences cannot be overcome by embracing all religions as variations on a single theme, because religions are exclusive: accepting one implies not accepting others. We may respect a religion or admire aspects of it, but to accept it fully requires conversion, for each religion claims to be correct in belief and practice, and these claims are in conflict. But what arguments can establish the truth of one religion and the falsity of all others?

As a test case consider Jainism, an ancient faith from India. It denies a creator God and is thus atheistic. Through self-mortification, its adherents seek to transcend the world and achieve a peace beyond all concerns. The central virtue is nonviolence against any living being. To this end all adherents must be vegetarians and cannot serve as butchers or soldiers. Its monks wear a gauze mask over the mouth to prevent the unintentional inhalation of an innocent insect. They are also required to sweep the ground in front of them as they walk, so as not to crush anything alive. They renounce all worldly attachments as well as any sexual pleasures, and they vow not to eat after sunset. If psychologically strong enough to achieve the goal of neglecting every personal interest, the monks commit suicide by self-starvation, thereby ridding the soul of all passions and bringing an appropriate close to an ethical life. The two main sects of the religion are divided over the question of whether the monks, to symbolize their complete renunciation of the material world, should practice nudity.

Can any argument demonstrate why Christianity, for example, is superior to Jainism? Granted, any one of their differing metaphysical and ethical principles could be isolated and subjected to critical scrutiny. But in view of their disagreements about so many fundamental matters, how could advocates for the two religions profitably debate their opposing outlooks and practices?

Note that an appeal to numbers would not settle the issue. Worldwide, Christianity has nearly 500 times as many adherents as Jainism, but Buddhism, Hinduism, and Islam together have hundreds of millions more adherents than Christianity. Whatever may be the relevance of such statistics to a sociologist of religion, they bear no philosophical significance. After all, at one time most people thought the sun went around the earth; nevertheless, this belief was false.

Some Christians might argue that the beliefs and practices of Jainism are too strange to be taken seriously. But how would the beliefs and practices of Christianity appear to Jains? What would they think of the immaculate conception, virgin birth, transubstantiation, and resurrection? What would they think of using a Roman device of torture as a central religious symbol? What would they think of the claim that the moral lapses of a person living today are forgiven because approximately two thousand years ago the son of God in the person of a Jewish teacher was put to death?

Each religion reflects the culture in which it develops, and cultures are not true or false, provable or disprovable, although one may be richer in some respects than another.

Yet a culture is not tested by arguments, nor are religions. They are less like scientific theories and more like works of art, not adding to our factual knowledge but enabling many to enrich their response to the challenges of the human condition.

Some have said that religions, regardless of the chasms between them, have been a force for good in human history. Hume, on the other hand, a leading historian as well as philosopher, forcefully expressed the opposite view, saying of religion: "Factions, civil wars, persecutions, subversions of government, oppression, slavery—these are the dismal consequences which always attend its prevalence over the minds of men. If the religious spirit be ever mentioned in any historical narration, we are sure to meet afterwards with a detail of the miseries which attend it."[2]

Surely the record of religion is mixed: sublime ideals and saintly acts are balanced by ignoble sentiments and horrendous practices. Religion as such is neither good nor evil. Religions have been both.

Religion Without God

IN THE PREVIOUS CHAPTER, I REFERRED TO RELIGIONS THAT DO not affirm the existence of God. Yet how is it possible for religious adherents to deny any concept of a deity separate from the natural world? Isn't it a contradiction to speak of religion without a supernatural God?

I propose to show that nothing in the theory or practice of religion—not ritual, not prayer, not metaphysical belief, not moral commitment—necessitates a commitment to theism. In other words, just as one may be a nonreligious theist, so one can be a religious agnostic or atheist.

Consider the concept of a ritual. It is a prescribed symbolic action. In the case of religion, the ritual is prescribed by the religious organization and the act symbolizes some aspect of religious belief. If the religion is supernaturalistic (that is, if it believes in a supernatural God), then those who reject such theology may, as a result, consider any ritual irrational. Yet although particular rituals may be based on irrational beliefs, nothing about the practice of ritual is inherently irrational.

Consider the act of two people shaking hands when meeting. This act is a ritual, prescribed by our society and symbolic of the individuals' mutual respect. The act is in no way irrational. If people shook hands in order to ward off evil demons, then shaking hands would indeed be irrational. But that reason is not why people shake hands. The ritual has no connection with God or demons but indicates the attitude one person has toward another.

It might be assumed that the ritual of handshaking escapes irrationality only because the ritual is not prescribed by any specific organization and is not part of an elaborate ceremony. To see that this assumption is false, consider the graduation ceremony at a college. The graduates and faculty members all wear peculiar hats and robes, and the participants stand and sit at appropriate times. The ceremony, however, is not at all irrational. Indeed, the rites of graduation day, far from being irrational, are symbolic of commitment to the process of education and the life of reason.

At first glance, rituals may seem a comparatively insignificant feature of life; yet they are a pervasive and treasured aspect of human experience. Who would want to eliminate the festivities associated with holidays such as Independence Day or Thanksgiving? What would college football be without songs, cheers, flags, and the innumerable other symbolic features surrounding the game? Those who disdain popular rituals typically proceed to establish their own distinctive ones, ranging from characteristic habits of dress to the use of drugs, symbolizing a rejection of traditional mores.

Religious persons, like all others, search for an appropriate means of emphasizing their commitment to a group or its values. Rituals provide such a means. Granted, supernaturalistic religion has often infused its rituals with superstition, but nonreligious rituals can be equally superstitious. For instance, most Americans view the Fourth of July as an occasion on which they can express pride in their country's heritage. With this purpose in mind, the holiday is one of great significance. However, if the singing of the fourth verse of "The Star-Spangled Banner" four times on the Fourth of July were thought to protect our country against future disasters, then the original meaning of the holiday would soon be lost in a maze of superstition.

A naturalistic (that is, nonsupernaturalistic) religion need not utilize ritual in a superstitious manner, because such a religion does not employ rituals to please a benevolent deity or appease an angry one. Rather, naturalistic religion views rituals, as one of its exponents has put it, as "the enhancement of life through the dramatization of great ideals."[1] If a group places great stress on justice or freedom, why should it not utilize ritual in order to emphasize these goals? Such a use of ritual serves to solidify the group and strengthen its devotion to its expressed purposes. These are buttressed if the ritual in question has the force of tradition, having been performed by many generations who have belonged to the same group and struggled to achieve the same goals. Ritual so conceived is not a form of superstition; rather, it is a reasonable means of strengthening religious commitment, as useful to naturalistic as to supernaturalistic religion.

Let us next turn to the concept of prayer. Some might suppose that naturalistic religion could have no use for prayer, because prayer is supposedly addressed to a supernatural being, and proponents of naturalistic religion do not believe in the existence of such a being. But this objection oversimplifies the concept of prayer, focusing attention on one type while neglecting an equally important but different sort.

Supernaturalistic religion makes extensive use of petitionary prayer, prayer that petitions a supernatural being for various favors. These may range from the personal happiness of the petitioner to the general welfare of all society. Because petitionary prayer rests on the assumption that a supernatural being exists, such prayer clearly has no place in a naturalistic religion.

Not all prayers, however, are prayers of petition. Some prayers are prayers of meditation. These are not directed to any supernatural being and are not requests for granting favors. Rather, these prayers provide the opportunity for persons to rethink their ultimate commitments and rededicate themselves to their ideals. Such prayers may take the form of silent devotion or involve oral repetition of certain central texts. Just as Americans repeat the Pledge of Allegiance and reread the Gettysburg Address, so adherents of naturalistic religion repeat the statements of their ideals and reread the documents that embody their traditional beliefs.

Granted, supernaturalistic religions, to the extent that they utilize prayers of meditation, tend to treat these prayers irrationally by supposing that if the prayers are not uttered a precise number of times under certain specific conditions, then the prayers lose all value. Yet prayer need not be viewed in this way. Rather, as the English biologist Sir Julian Huxley (1887–1975) wrote, prayer "permits the bringing before the mind of a world of thought which in most people must inevitably be absent during the occupation of ordinary life. . . . [I]t is the means by which the mind may fix itself upon this or that noble or beautiful or awe-inspiring idea, and so grow to it and come to realize it more fully."[2]

Such a use of prayer may be enhanced by song, instrumental music, and various types of symbolism. These elements, fused together, provide the means for adherents of naturalistic religion to engage in religious services akin to those engaged in by adherents of supernaturalistic religion. The difference between the two services is that those who participate in the latter come to relate themselves to God, whereas those who participate in the former come to relate themselves to their fellow human beings and the world in which we live.

Thus far we have examined how ritual and prayer can be utilized in naturalistic religion, but to adopt a religious perspective also involves metaphysical beliefs and moral commitments. Can these be maintained without recourse to supernaturalism?

If we use the term *metaphysics* in its usual sense, referring to the systematic study of the most basic features of existence, then a metaphysical system may be either supernaturalistic or naturalistic. Representative of a supernaturalistic theory are the views of the influential French philosopher and scientist René Descartes (1596–1650) and the illustrious German philosopher and mathematician Gottfried Leibniz (1646–1716). Representative of a naturalistic theory are the views of the eminent Dutch philosopher Baruch Spinoza (1632–1677) and the only person ever named honorary president for life of the American Philosophical Association, John Dewey.

Spinoza's *Ethics,* for example, one of the greatest of all metaphysical works, explicitly rejects the view that any being exists apart from Nature itself. Spinoza identifies God with Nature as a whole and urges that the good life consists in coming to understand Nature. In his words, "our salvation, or blessedness, or freedom consists in a constant and eternal love toward God."[3] Spinoza's concept of God, however, is explicitly not the supernaturalistic concept of God, and Spinoza's metaphysical system thus exemplifies not only a naturalistic metaphysics but also the possibility of reinterpreting the concept of God within a naturalistic framework.

Can those who do not believe in a supernaturalistic God commit themselves to moral principles, or is the acceptance of moral principles dependent on the acceptance of supernaturalism? Some have assumed that those who reject a supernaturalistic God are necessarily immoral, for their denial of the existence of such a God leaves them free to act without fear of divine punishment. This assumption, however, is seriously mistaken.

The refutation of the view that morality must rest on belief in a supernatural God was provided more than two thousand years ago in Plato's remarkable dialogue, the *Euthyphro*. Plato's teacher, Socrates, who in most of Plato's works is given the leading role, asks the overconfident Euthyphro the following question: Are actions right because God says they are right, or does God say actions are right because they are right? This question is not a verbal trick; on the contrary, it poses a serious dilemma for those who believe in a supernatural deity.

Socrates was inquiring whether actions are right because of God's fiat or whether God is Himself subject to moral standards. If actions are right because of God's command, then anything God commands is right, including torture or murder. Some may accept this discomforting view, but then their assertion that God is good becomes pointless, for if the good is whatever God commands, to say that God commands rightly is simply to say that He commands as He commands, which is a tautology. This approach makes a mockery of morality, for might does not make right, even if the might is the infinite might of God. To act morally is not to act out of fear of punishment; it is not to act as one is commanded to act. Rather, it is to act as one ought to act, and how one ought to act is not dependent on anyone's power, even if the power be divine.

Thus actions are not right because God commands them; on the contrary, God commands them because they are right. What is right is independent of what God commands, for what He commands must conform with an independent standard in order to be right. Because one could act intentionally in accord with this independent standard without believing in the existence of a supernatural God, it follows that morality does not rest on supernaturalism. Consequently, naturalists can be highly moral (as well as immoral) persons, and supernaturalists can be highly immoral (as well as moral) persons. This conclusion should come as no surprise to anyone who has contrasted the benevolent life of the inspiring teacher Buddha (563–483 B.C.E.), an atheist, with the malevolent life of the churchman Tomás de Torquemada (1420–1498), who devised and enforced the unimaginable cruelties of the Spanish Inquisition.

We have now seen that naturalistic religion is a genuine possibility, since reasonable individuals may perform rituals, utter prayers, accept metaphysical beliefs, and commit themselves to moral principles without believing in supernaturalism. Indeed, even a supernaturalistic religion such as Christianity or Judaism may be reinterpreted to eliminate any commitment to supernaturalism. Consider, for example, those Christians who accept the "Death of God"[4] or those Jews who belong to the influential Reconstructionist movement in Judaism.[5]

Such options are philosophically respectable. Whether to choose any of them is for each person to decide.

C H A P T E R   14

Heaven and Hell

ONE FEATURE OF SOME SUPERNATURALIST RELIGIONS, INCLUDING traditional Christianity and Islam, is the belief that life on earth is followed by an afterlife in which some persons abide forever in a place of joy while others endure everlasting suffering in a place of doom. Many people find these visions compelling and therefore embrace a religion that emphasizes them. But are the concepts of heaven and hell viable?

They raise more questions than they resolve. Why should finite wickedness deserve infinite punishment? Why should finite goodness deserve infinite reward? Is heaven reserved for adherents of only one religion? Are all other believers assigned to hell? What is the fate of those who lived before the development of any particular religion? Are they condemned to hell for not believing in a doctrine that had not yet been formulated when they lived? What about infants who die? How are they to be judged? What about beloved dogs, cats, and other creatures who have enriched the lives of so many persons? Might some of these animals merit a place in heaven? If not, how joyful can heaven be for those deprived of their faithful companions?

This last question is explored in "The Hunt," a provocative episode of the award-winning television series *The Twilight Zone.* An old hillbilly named Simpson and his hound dog Rip appear to drown in a backwoods pond but awake the next morning near the water, walk toward the local graveyard, come to an unfamiliar fence, follow it, and arrive at a gate. The gatekeeper explains to Simpson that he is at the entrance to heaven. He is welcome, but Rip is not; no dogs are allowed. Simpson becomes infuriated, declaring that he would rather stay with Rip than go to heaven, and man and dog walk away together. Soon they meet an angel sent to accompany them to heaven. Simpson protests that he won't go without Rip, and the angel tells Simpson that Rip is welcome in heaven. The angel explains that if Simpson had left Rip and gone through the gate, he would have made a terrible mistake, for the gatekeeper had lied: the gate was the entrance to hell. Why had Rip been excluded? He would have smelled the brimstone and warned Simpson away. As the angel says, "You see, Mr. Simpson, a man, well he'll walk right into Hell with both eyes open—but even the Devil can't fool a dog!"[1]

The effectiveness of this story depends in part on our being able to envision hell but not heaven. For when we realize that Simpson nearly made the mistake of going to hell, we can easily imagine the horrors that awaited him. We all are familiar with the nature of misery. Who among us has not known sorrow or suffering? Most have experienced anguish and agony. Too many have suffered tortures of mind and body. Could the horrors of hell be worse than those suffered by many in their dreadful lives on earth? I doubt it. As the visionary English poet William Blake (1757–1827) wrote,

Every Night & every Morn
Some to Misery are Born.
Every Morn & every Night
Some are Born to sweet delight.
Some are Born to sweet delight,
Some are Born to Endless Night.[2]

Those born on earth to endless night might welcome whatever hell offers.

Heaven, however, defies description. What events take place there? How do individuals relate to each other? What activities occupy them? A familiar supposition is that harps are played, but how long can harp music suffice for felicity? We understand the happiness that Rip brings Simpson. But how does it compare to the joys Simpson would experience in heaven? Not knowing, we are comfortable with Simpson rejecting heaven and staying with Rip.

To see additional difficulties involved in grasping the concept of heaven, consider the case of Willie Mays, the spectacular baseball player whose greatest joy was to play the game he loved. What does heaven offer him? Presumably bats, balls, and gloves are not found there. So what does Willie Mays do? Assuming he is the same person who made that spectacular catch in the 1954 World Series, how can the delights that supposedly await him in heaven match those he knew on earth?

Furthermore, some of Mays's fans found their greatest delight in watching him play baseball. Won't they be denied this joy in heaven? Whatever heaven may offer them, they will miss watching Willie in action.

The problems mount. Consider two individuals, Peters and Peterson, and suppose that Peters looks forward to the joy of spending eternity with Peterson, whereas Peterson looks forward to the joy of being forever free of Peters. Assuming they retain their distinctive personalities, including their fundamental likes and dislikes, how can they both attain heavenly bliss?

More questions arise in attempting to understand the supposition that our bodies will be resurrected. Will they appear as they did when we were ten, forty, or eighty years old? If a person suffered from diabetes, will the resurrected body suffer from the disease? In what sense would a resurrected person be identical to the person who died? If a ship is destroyed and an identical one is built, the second is a different ship from the first. Similarly, if a person is destroyed and an identical one is created, the second is a different person from the first.

One way to avoid these difficulties is to suppose that after death what survives are not bodies but souls. Thus although Simpson appeared to have a body, in reality he was only a soul. Was Rip also a soul, or do dogs not have souls? Can two souls inhabit a single body, or is it one soul to a customer?

What, after all, is a soul? Supposedly, when added to a body, a soul converts that body into a person. Does the soul itself think and feel? In that case, it is already a person and needs no body. If it doesn't think and feel, how does it start to do so when it enters a body?

This problem can be avoided by recognizing that some bodies can think and feel. They do so as a result of possessing brains, which are physical objects and not immaterial souls. Yet brains cease functioning. People die.

Despite all the conceptual difficulties, some may continue to believe in heaven and hell. But given the bewildering questions that make it difficult to provide a persuasive, or even coherent, account of survival in a next world, trying to imagine such a possible state of affairs provides no help in enabling us to understand our lives in the world we actually inhabit.

C H A P T E R 15

Life Without God

AN ASSUMPTION COMMON TO MANY THEISTS IS THAT IF WE DO not believe in the existence of God, our life is somehow diminished. Why accept this view? After all, even if God does not exist, we are still alive, as are others we cherish, we still experience times of health and sickness, we still strive to achieve goals, we still relish successes and regret failures, we still witness inspiring acts of goodness and disheartening deeds of evil, and we still face moral problems and have to make difficult decisions.

Granted, we cannot expect help from God. But even if He exists, our choices are our own, not His. We cannot look to God for guidance, because what He wills is unknown.

We cannot rest secure in the belief that God is taking care of us, because in any case bad things happen to good people, and good things happen to bad people.

Would life without God lack meaning? The answer depends on what sort of meaning a life can have. If a meaningful life is one in which each individual plays a role in a divine drama, entering and exiting the stage at an appointed time in order to serve God's purposes, then in the absence of God, life has no meaning.

Why assume that people cannot have their own purposes, independent of any divine playwright? Suppose I wish to devote my life to teaching philosophy, you wish to devote your life to providing medical care to the sick, and others wish to devote their lives to composing music, cultivating a garden, or raising a family. Why aren't these activities meaningful? None of them depends on the existence of God. They nevertheless provide life with significance. They are freely chosen, not preordained, but so much the better. They are expressions of our own personalities and values.

Or is the problem supposed to be that in the absence of God, we are unable to decide which values or moral principles to accept? This problem can be solved by using reason to assess specific value judgments in the light of shared human concerns and our common experience.

To illustrate the process, let us examine in turn various ethical principles that have been thought by many to embody the will of God but that, regardless of whether God exists, fall short of providing an entirely satisfactory foundation for morality. These rules, whatever their origin, are not immune from difficulties that can be recognized by theists and nontheists alike. Both groups can assess such moral guidelines.

Consider the Golden Rule, a moral principle endorsed by various religious traditions, both theistic and nontheistic. Its positive formulation, attributed to Jesus, is: "In everything do to others as you would have them do to you."[1] The negative formulation, which appeared five centuries earlier, is attributed to the Chinese sage Confucius (c. 551–479 B.C.E.) and was later proposed by the Jewish scholar Hillel (c. 30 B.C.E.–10 C.E.) The latter put it as follows: "What is hateful to you, do not to your neighbor."[2] Is either of these versions entirely acceptable?

Consider first the positive formulation. Granted, we should usually treat others as we would wish them to treat us. For instance, we should go to the aid of an injured person, just as we would wish that person to come to our aid if we were injured. If we always followed this rule, however, the results would be unfortunate. Consider masochists, who derive pleasure from being hurt. Were they to act according to the principle in question, their duty would be to inflict pain, thereby doing to others as they wish done to themselves. Similarly, consider a person who enjoys receiving telephone calls, regardless of who is calling. The principle would require that person to telephone everyone, thereby reciprocating preferred treatment. Indeed, strictly speaking, to fulfill the positive formulation of the Golden Rule would be impossible because we wish so many others to do so much for us that we would not have time to do all that is necessary to treat them likewise. As the German-born philosopher Walter Kaufman (1921–1980) commented, "anyone who tried to live up to Jesus's rule would become an insufferable nuisance."[3]

In this respect the negative formulation of the Golden Rule is preferable because it does not imply that we have innumerable duties toward everyone else. Neither does it imply that masochists ought to inflict pain on others, nor that those who enjoy receiving telephone calls ought themselves to make calls. However, while the negative formulation does not require these actions, neither does it forbid them. It enjoins us not to do to others what is hateful to ourselves, but pain is not hateful to the masochist and calls are not hateful to the telephone enthusiast. Thus the negative formulation of the Golden Rule, though superior in one way to the positive formulation, is not without weakness, because it does not prohibit actions that ought to be prohibited.

Whether the Golden Rule in either formulation is supposed to be of divine origin makes no difference in its assessment. Whatever its source, all can agree that it does not by itself serve as the ultimate moral touchstone.

The Ten Commandments, accepted by adherents of a variety of religions, also have their limitations. Consider the Second Commandment, which, after prohibiting the making or serving of sculptured images, goes on to say, "For I the LORD your God am an impassioned God, visiting the guilt of the parents upon the children, upon the third and upon the fourth generations of those who reject Me, but showing kindness to the thousandth generation of those who love Me and keep My commandments."[4] But to punish one person for the moral lapses of another is unethical, as is rewarding a person for the good deeds done by another. This point was made emphatically by the prophet Ezekiel, who declared: "A child shall not share the burden of a parent's guilt, nor shall a parent share the burden of a child's guilt; the righteousness of the righteous shall be accounted to him alone, and the wickedness of the wicked shall be accounted to him alone."[5] Incidentally, Ezekiel's principles rule out the possibility that anyone, including God, could act in such a way as to absolve us of responsibility for our failings. Only we as individuals can atone for our own errors.

The Fifth Commandment instructs individuals to honor their father and mother. Suppose, however, parents break the Second Commandment by making and worshipping sculptured images. Or perhaps they break some of the remaining commandments by coveting a neighbor's property, bearing false witness, stealing, engaging in adultery, or even committing murder. Although they might still merit their child's concern, parents who acted in such ways would not deserve to be honored.

Two of the commandments take slavery for granted. The Fourth, which requires individuals to remember the Sabbath day and keep it holy, prohibits work at that time by "you, your son or daughter, your male or female slave."[6] The Tenth prohibits coveting anything that belongs to a neighbor, including his "wife, or his male or female slave."[7] Slavery we all now agree is immoral, yet the Ten Commandments treat it as an acceptable practice.

A further problem is that the commandments are stated as if they allowed no exceptions. Yet under certain circumstances, not to break a commandment would be widely regarded as unethical. For example, if a young girl's life depended on her mother's stealing a small amount of money from a wealthy, immoral person, most of us would view the theft favorably.

Not only do certain circumstances call for making exceptions to the commandments, but situations can develop in which fulfilling one commandment would amount to breaking another. If, for instance, a man had to work on the Sabbath in order to take his critically ill father to the hospital, the commandment to honor one's father and mother would take precedence over the commandment not to work on the Sabbath. The commandments have exceptions, but do not themselves provide any guidance for when or how to make such exceptions. Thus regardless of claims of their divine origin and despite their moral worth, the Ten Commandments fall short as an ultimate guide to morality.

The same is true of that sacred Christian text, the Sermon on the Mount. Amid its beauties of language and thought, we find such an unacceptable principle as "[I]f your right hand causes you to sin, cut it off and throw it away . . ."[8] Any statement, of course, can be interpreted to render it sensible, but taken literally, thieves cutting off their hands would be acts of lunacy. If the statement is not to be taken literally, however, it does not provide an unambiguous guide to moral action.

A similar problem is implicit in Jesus's instruction that "whoever marries a divorced woman commits adultery."[9] Few would find such a principle morally acceptable. What of Jesus's saying, "[D]o not worry about your life, what you will eat or what you will drink . . ."[10] Wouldn't such a lack of concern for oneself be a sign of a psychological problem as well as an unfair drain on family and friends?

If these sayings appear peripheral to Jesus's principal message, consider this central passage: "Do not resist an evildoer. But if anyone strikes you on the right cheek, turn the other also; and if anyone wants to sue you and take your coat, give your cloak as well . . ."[11] The difficulty with such pacifism is that those who adhere to it depend on others' not adhering to it in order to avoid the triumph of evil. Turning the other cheek to a Hitler is death. Not to fight for the right is wrong. Throughout history, when those who consider themselves devout Christians have come under attack, they have temporarily put aside the Sermon on the Mount and picked up their weapons. To have done otherwise would have led to the destruction of Christianity. Recall that when Jesus entered Jerusalem, he "drove out all who were selling and buying in the temple, and he overturned the tables of the money changers and the seats of those who sold doves."[12] So much for turning the other cheek.

Over the course of centuries many persons have found the Golden Rule, the Ten Commandments, or the Sermon on the Mount inspirational and worthy of devotion. Yet these statements of principle, like all others, require interpretation by the use of reason and testing by appeal to the lessons of experience. If God exists, our principles, even if attributed to the divine, still need to be evaluated. Theism doesn't solve our moral problems. And even if God does not exist, we may still commit ourselves to care for others. A world without God need not be a world without love.

A Religious Life

MANY SUPPOSE THAT A RELIGIOUS LIFE NECESSARILY INVOLVES believing in God, doing what is right in order to serve God's will, and hoping thereby to attain the bliss supposedly found in heaven. I propose instead that someone may lead a religious life without believing in God, but by doing what is right in response to the needs of others, thereby potentially achieving the joys that can be found on earth.

For illustration, I turn to a Yiddish tale authored by the eminent Polish writer I. L. Peretz (1852–1915), described by one notable critic as "arguably the most important figure in the development of modern Jewish culture."[1] To summarize the story would fail to do it justice, and so I present it in its entirety.[2]

If Not Higher

Early every Friday morning, at the time of the Penitential Prayers,[3] the rabbi of Nemirov[4] would vanish.

He was nowhere to be seen—neither in the synagogue nor in the two study houses nor at a minyan.[5] And he was certainly not at home. His door stood open: whoever wished could go in and out; no one would steal from the rabbi. But not a living creature was within.

Where could the rabbi be? Where should he be? In heaven, no doubt. A rabbi has plenty of business to take care of just before the Days of Awe.[6] Jews, God bless them, need livelihood, peace, health, and good matches. They want to be pious and good, but our sins are so great, and Satan of the thousand eyes watches the whole earth from one end to the other. What he sees, he reports; he denounces, informs. Who can help us if not the rabbi!

That's what the people thought.

But once a Litvak[7] came, and he laughed. You know the Litvaks. They think little of the holy books but stuff themselves with Talmud[8] and law. So this Litvak points to a passage in the Gemara—it sticks in your eyes—where it is written that even Moses our Teacher did not ascend to heaven during his lifetime but remained suspended two and a half feet below. Go argue with a Litvak!

So where can the rabbi be?

"That's not my business," said the Litvak, shrugging. Yet all the while—what a Litvak can do!—he is scheming to find out.

That same night, right after the evening prayers, the Litvak steals into the rabbi's room, slides under the rabbi's bed, and waits. He'll watch all night and discover where the rabbi vanishes and what he does during the Penitential Prayers.

Someone else might have gotten drowsy and fallen asleep, but a Litvak is never at a loss; he recites a whole tractate of the Talmud by heart.

At dawn he hears the call to prayers.

The rabbi has already been awake for a long time. The Litvak has heard him groaning for a whole hour.

Whoever has heard the rabbi of Nemirov groan knows how much sorrow for all Israel, how much suffering, lies in each groan. A man's heart might break, hearing it. But a Litvak is made of iron; he listens and remains where he is. The rabbi—long life to him!—lies on the bed, and the Litvak under the bed.

Then the Litvak hears the beds in the house begin to creak; he hears people jumping out of their beds, mumbling a few Jewish words, pouring water on their fingernails, banging doors. Everyone has left. It is again quiet and dark; a bit of light from the moon shines through the shutters.

(Afterward, the Litvak admitted that when he found himself alone with the rabbi a great fear took hold of him. Goose pimples spread across his skin, and the roots of his sidelocks pricked him like needles. A trifle: to be alone with the rabbi at the time of the Penitential Prayers! But a Litvak is stubborn. So he quivered like a fish in water and remained where he was.)

Finally the rabbi—long life to him!—arises. First, he does what befits a Jew.[9] Then he goes to the clothes closet and takes out a bundle of peasant clothes: linen trousers, high boots, a coat, a big felt hat, and a long, wide leather belt studded with brass nails. The rabbi gets dressed. From his coat pocket dangles the end of a heavy peasant rope.

The rabbi goes out, and the Litvak follows him.

On the way the rabbi stops in the kitchen, bends down, takes an ax from under the bed, puts it into his belt, and leaves the house. The Litvak trembles but continues to follow.

The hushed dread of the Days of Awe hangs over the dark streets. Every once in a while a cry rises from some minyan reciting the Penitential Prayers, or from a sickbed. The rabbi hugs the sides of the streets, keeping to the shade of the houses. He glides from house to house, and the Litvak after him. The Litvak hears the sound of his heartbeats mingling with the sound of the rabbi's heavy steps. But he keeps on going and follows the rabbi to the outskirts of the town.

A small wood stands just outside the town.

The rabbi—long life to him!—enters the wood. He takes thirty or forty steps and stops by a small tree. The Litvak, overcome with amazement, watches the rabbi take the ax out of his belt and strike the tree. He hears the tree creak and fall. The rabbi chops the tree into logs and the logs into sticks. Then he makes a bundle of the wood and ties it with the rope in his pocket. He puts the bundle of wood on his back, shoves the ax back into his belt, and returns to the town.

He stops at a back street beside a small, broken-down shack and knocks at the window.

"Who is there?" asks a frightened voice. The Litvak recognizes it as the voice of a sick Jewish woman.

"I," answers the rabbi in the accent of a peasant.

"Who is I?"

Again the rabbi answers in Russian. "Vassil."

"Who is Vassil, and what do you want?"

"I have wood to sell, very cheap." And not waiting for the woman's reply, he goes into the house.

The Litvak steals in after him. In the gray light of early morning he sees a poor room with broken, miserable furnishings. A sick woman, wrapped in rags, lies on the bed. She complains bitterly, "Buy? How can I buy? Where will a poor widow get money?"

"I'll lend it to you," answers the supposed Vassil. "It's only six cents."

"And how will I ever pay you back?" asks the poor woman, groaning.

"Foolish one," says the rabbi reproachfully. "See, you are a poor, sick Jew, and I am ready to trust you with a little wood. I am sure you'll pay. While you, you have such a great and mighty God and you don't trust him for six cents."

"And who will kindle the fire?" asks the widow. "Have I the strength to get up? My son is at work."

"I'll kindle the fire," answers the rabbi.

As the rabbi put the wood into the oven he recited, in a groan, the first portion of the Penitential Prayers.

As he kindled the fire and the wood burned brightly, he recited, a bit more joyously, the second portion of the Penitential Prayers. When the fire was set, he recited the third portion, and then he shut the stove.

The Litvak who saw all this became a disciple of the rabbi.

And ever after, when another disciple tells how the rabbi of Nemirov ascends to heaven at the time of the Penitential Prayers, the Litvak does not laugh. He only adds quietly, "If not higher."

Those last three words embody a view of God, reason, and religion. If the Litvak believed in God and His heaven, he could conceive nothing higher. His comment thus signifies a skeptical attitude toward traditional theism. Yet he becomes a follower of the rabbi because of admiration for the rabbi's ethical commitments and the extraordinary manner in which he fulfills them.

The rabbi is not without guile. He acts surreptitiously, dons a disguise, and speaks misleadingly to the distressed woman. But the deceptions serve a moral purpose, and in striving to do good the rabbi is not bound by ordinary conventions. He does not slavishly follow the law but seeks to embody its spirit.

The rabbi thereby captures the essence of a religion that can be embraced even by those who do not adopt orthodox theistic beliefs. It has its rituals and prayers, but these are valuable only insofar as they lead to noble deeds. Whether to affirm the existence of God or Satan is a metaphysical question about which the rabbi and the Litvak may disagree. (Who knows what the cunning rabbi believes?) The rabbi's eminence, however, rests not on the profundity of his theology but on the deep concern he shows for the sick and the poor. His wondrous actions lead the Litvak to be in awe of the rabbi's holiness.

Belief in God, the divine will, and the promise of eternal life are important aspects of many religions, but not all. The Litvak is a doubter but becomes a disciple. He laughs at the Bible but eventually reveres the rabbi. The Litvak scoffs at talk of heaven, but as events unfold his understanding grows. In the end the Litvak realizes that without ever leaving this world the rabbi in his wisdom has found a way to deal with suffering and has attained a blessedness that lies beyond any celestial vision of which human beings may dream.

Introduction

1. *Four Films of Woody Allen: Annie Hall, Interiors, Manhattan, Stardust Memories* (New York: Random House, 1982), p. 366.
2. David Hume, *Dialogues Concerning Natural Religion* (New York: Oxford University Press, 1998), part XII.

1. Proving God's Existence?

1. *The Later Works of John Dewey, 1925–1953,* vol. 9, ed. Jo Ann Boydston (Carbondale: Southern Illinois University Press, 1988), p. 34.
2. My use of "His" is not intended to imply that God is masculine.
3. Hume, part VI.
4. Ibid., part V.
5. George Berkeley, *A Treatise Concerning the Principles of Human Knowledge* (Indianapolis: Hackett Publishing Company, 1982), sec. 146.
6. Hume, part X.

2. The Problem of Evil

1. John Hick, *Philosophy of Religion,* 4th ed. (Englewood Cliffs, NJ: Prentice-Hall, 1990), pp. 39–48.

3. The Problem of Goodness

1. My use of "He" is not intended to imply that the Demon is masculine.

4. The Moriarty Hypothesis

1. Arthur Conan Doyle, *The Complete Sherlock Holmes* (Garden City, NY: Doubleday, n.d.), pp. 471, 496, 769. The works cited are "The Final Problem," "The Adventure of the Norwood Builder," and "The Valley of Fear."
2. Doyle, "The Adventure of the Retired Colourman," p. 1113.
3. Hume, part X.
4. I Corinthians 13:12. The translation is from *The Holy Bible: New Revised Standard Version* (New York and Oxford: Oxford University Press, 1989).
5. Doyle, "The Final Problem," p. 471.
6. Ecclesiastes 4:2–3. The translation is from *Tanakh: The Holy Scriptures* (Philadelphia: Jewish Publication Society, 1988).

5. Dummy Hypotheses

1. Anita Shreve, *All He Ever Wanted* (Boston: Little, Brown and Company, 2003), p. 79.
2. Devotees of Sherlock Holmes will recall that a dummy bell rope is a critical clue in Sir Arthur Conan Doyle's masterful story, "The Adventure of the Speckled Band."

7. Skepticism about Faith

1. Mortimer J. Cohen, *Pathways through the Bible* (Philadelphia: Jewish Publication Society of America, 1946), p. 460.
2. Jack J. Cohen, *The Case for Religious Naturalism* (New York: The Reconstructionist Press, 1958), p. 83.
3. David Trueblood, *The Logic of Belief* (New York: Harper & Brothers, 1942), pp. 293–294.

8. The Problem of Meaning

1. I take the term from Lewis Carroll's humorous poem "The Hunting of the Snark: An Agony, in Eight Fits." It concludes: "For the Snark *was* a Boojum, you see," thus explaining one unknown concept in terms of another and leaving both without sense.
2. Levi ben Gershom, *The Wars of the Lord,* trans. Seymour Feldman (Philadelphia: Jewish Publication Society, 1987), vol. 2, p. 111.
3. Janet Martin Soskice, *Metaphor and Religious Language* (Oxford: Clarendon Press, 1985), p. 57.
4. Ibid., pp. 57–58.
5. Ibid., p. 101.
6. Ibid., p. 140.

9. Miracles

1. A fiery chariot takes Elijah to heaven. See II Kings 2:11.
2. David Hume, *An Enquiry Concerning Human Understanding* (New York: Oxford University Press, 1995), part X.

10. God Without Religion

1. David Hume, *A Treatise of Human Nature* (New York: Oxford University Press, 1978), III, 1, 1.
2. Sidney Hook, *The Quest for Being* (New York: St. Martin's, 1961), pp. 130–131.

11. Playing the Odds

1. See Blaise Pascal, *Pensées and Other Writings,* trans. Honor Levi (New York: Oxford University Press, 1995), pp. 152–156.
2. Benjamin Franklin, *Poor Richard's Almanack,* 1736.
3. Amos 5:21–24.

12. Religions

1. I rely throughout this chapter on Ninian Smart, *The Religious Experience of Mankind* (New York: Charles Scribner's Sons, 1969).
2. Hume, *Dialogues Concerning Natural Religion*, part XII.

13. Religion Without God

1. Jack J. Cohen, *The Case for Religious Naturalism*, p. 150.
2. Julian Huxley, *Religion without Revelation* (New York: New American Library, 1957), p. 141.
3. Baruch Spinoza, *Ethics*, ed. James Gutmann (New York: Hafner, 1957), part V, prop. 36, note.
4. See John H. T. Robinson, *Honest to God* (Philadelphia: Westminster, 1963).
5. See Mordecai M. Kaplan, *Judaism as a Civilization* (New York: Schocken, 1967).

14. Heaven and Hell

1. Marc Scott Zicree, *The Twilight Zone Companion* (New York: Bantam Books, 1982), pp. 242–244.
2. William Blake, *Auguries of Innocence*, lines 119–124. "Endless Night" is the title of one of Agatha Christie's finest novels.

15. Life Without God

1. Matthew 7:12.
2. *The Babylonian Talmud* (London: Soncino Press, 1938), Shabbath, 31a.
3. Walter Kaufman, *The Faith of a Heretic* (New York: Doubleday, 1963), p. 212.
4. Exodus 20:5–6.
5. Ezekiel 18:20.

6. Exodus 20:10.
7. Exodus 20:14.
8. Matthew 5:30.
9. Matthew 5:32.
10. Matthew 6:25.
11. Matthew 5:39.
12. Matthew 21:12.

16. A Religious Life

1. *The I. L. Peretz Reader,* ed. Ruth R. Wisse (New Haven and London: Yale University Press, 2002), xiii.
2. "If Not Higher" by I. L. Peretz, translated by Marie Syrkin, from *A Treasury of Yiddish Stories* by Irving Howe and Eliezer Greenberg, editors, copyright © 1953, 1954, 1989 by Viking Penguin, renewed © 1981, 1982 by Irving Howe and Eliezer Greenberg. Used by permission of Viking Penguin, a division of Penguin Group (USA), Inc. The accompanying notes are my own.
3. A type of liturgical poetry requesting forgiveness from sin.
4. A Ukrainian city with a flourishing Jewish community in the seventeenth century but the scene of a ghastly massacre of the Jews by the Cossacks in 1648.
5. A group of ten male adult Jews, the minimum required for a communal prayer.
6. The ten-day period from Rosh Hashonah, the Jewish New Year, to Yom Kippur, the Day of Atonement.
7. A Jew from Lithuania.
8. The multi-volume compilation of Jewish law and commentary, containing the Mishnah, the core of the Oral Law, and the Gemara, a supplement to the Mishnah.
9. Morning prayers.

Steven M. Cahn is Professor of Philosophy at the Graduate Center of The City University of New York, where he served as Provost and Vice President for Academic Affairs and then as Acting President.

He received his A.B. from Columbia College and his Ph.D. from Columbia University. He has taught at Dartmouth College, Vassar College, the University of Rochester, New York University, and the University of Vermont, where he headed the Department of Philosophy. He has also served as a program officer at the Exxon Education Foundation, acting director for humanities at The Rockefeller Foundation, and director of the Division of General Programs at the National Endowment for the Humanities. He chaired the American Philosophical Association's Committee on the Teaching of Philosophy and is President of the John Dewey Foundation.

Among the eight books Professor Cahn has authored are *Fate, Logic, and Time; Saints and Scamps: Ethics in Academia, Revised Edition;* and *Puzzles & Perplexities: Collected Essays.* He has edited or co-edited twenty-four books, including *Classics of Western Philosophy, Sixth Edition; Contemporary Philosophy of Religion; Questions About God: Today's Philosophers Ponder the Divine; Ten Essential Texts in the Philosophy of Religion: Classics and Contemporary Issues; Exploring Philosophy: An Introductory Anthology, Second Edition;* and *Philosophical Horizons: Introductory Readings.*

His numerous articles have appeared in such varied publications as *The Journal of Philosophy, The Chronicle of Higher Education, Shakespeare Quarterly, The American Journal of Medicine, The Journal of Aesthetics and Art Criticism, The New Republic,* and *The New York Times.*

INDEX